GOSPEL REFLECTIONS
FOR MINDS & HEARTS

10
MINUTES

It is surely right that in any pursuit of greater understanding of the heart of God, one begins with the Scriptures.

So it is that in a series of 10-minute gospel reflections that will stir the imagination, Peter Malone msc offers a distillation of various moments of encounter in Jesus' life together with some key passages from the Hebrew Scriptures that shed light on the Gospel moment and enable the reader to enter more fully into it; then to embark on a gentle journey of both mind and heart—one that is enticing for the author's tender, and at times humorously refreshing insights and perspectives that form the lens through which the theme of each chapter is presented. And, of course, the *Visio Divina* lens in which Peter is so immersed and able to share with the reader brings an added richness to the collection.

In this way, the reader is drawn to look upon, listen to and dwell on the words and actions of the human Jesus of the gospels, and all they reveal about Jesus' heart—and thus, what we can know of the ever-alluring mystery of the heart of God.

This collection is a delightful synthesis of treasures that quite naturally invites the reader into prayerful reflection—treasures that truly will stimulate minds and move hearts.

Anne McAtomney,
Director
Chevalier Institute, Kensington.

Fr Peter Malone's latest book *10 Minutes* is an engaging work of gospel reflections that carries the reader along through telling anecdotes and cinematic representations. Peter integrates the story of Jesus with the experiences of various characters and their faith journeys, making Jesus' life and his humanity tangible. Who wouldn't fall in love with a friend like that? The book is an excellent resource for educators looking to 'fill young minds with knowledge, yes, but more important, give those minds a compass so that that knowledge doesn't go to waste (Principal Jacobs - *Mr Holland's Opus*). Peter's insightful reflections and contemporary images create a space where a broad audience can encounter Jesus' life and values in dialogue with their own experience. *10 Minutes* is a delightful invitation to get to know Jesus more personally and make meaning for one's life.

Helena Goldsmith,
Catholic Mission and Identity
Melbourne Archdiocese Catholic Schools (MACS).

Peter Malone's *10 Minutes: Gospel reflections for minds and hearts* lingers much longer in our conscious and sub-conscious minds. Vignettes with titles such as *Jesus, stand-up comedian* and *Jesus splashes his mother* draw us in to affirm what Malone describes as the purpose of the book: 'The Gospel reflections are to stimulate our minds and our understanding as well as move our hearts and our emotions'. Firmly rooted in scripture, laced with literary and cinematic references and journeying down the path of *Visio Divina* (*Spiritual Watching*), the 20 essays on life and faith will make us ponder, smile and read them again, and again.

Paul Beirne,
Emeritus Professor (University of Divinity)
Director
Heart of Life Centre for Spiritual and Pastoral Formation, Malvern.

GOSPEL REFLECTIONS
FOR MINDS & HEARTS

10
MINUTES

PETER MALONE

COVENTRY
PRESS

Published in Australia by
Coventry Press
33 Scoresby Road
Bayswater VIC 3153

ISBN 9781922589095

Scripture quotations are from the *Jerusalem Bible* copyright © 1966 by Darton
Longman & Todd Ltd and Doubleday and Company Ltd.

Catalogue-in-Publication entry is available from the National Library
of Australia http://catalogue.nla.gov.au

Cover design by Ian James – www.jgd.com.au
Text design by Coventry Press
Set in EBGaramond

Printed in Australia

Contents

Foreword   9

Jesus according to the Scriptures   11

Write your own Gospel   14

The Calling of Prophets   17

Spirituality of Apostles, Evangelisers   20

Jesus and his Encounters   24

Jesus' Friends   27

Jesus Heals   30

A Perspective on Discipleship   33

Jesus and a Justice Charter   35

Jesus' Story of the (Most) Permissive Father   37

Jesus: Man with no Name   40

The New and Everlasting Covenant   43

Speaking of Jesus' Resurrection   46

Jonah: Odd Prophet Out   49

Jesus as Stand-up Comedian   53

Jesus Splashes his Mother   56

Imaging the Tempter   59

Mary Mother, Mary Prophet   62

Mary Growing Older   65

My Jesus Film/your Jesus Film   68

And then...   71

Foreword

Welcome to the world of Jesus according to the Scriptures.

And the title? The 10 minutes? That is the time, more or less, that it takes to read a chapter. But it will lead to a second 10 minutes, and another... time to reflect on the theme, to pray the theme.

The author taught an introduction course on the Old Testament, the Jewish Scriptures, which led to a course on The New Testament in the light of the Old. That is what is behind this book, an opportunity to look at passages, stories of Jesus, some familiar, some perhaps not, but to appreciate them more in the light of the Old. (There are some chapters focusing on aspects of the Old Testament but you will see why.)

It is useful to remind ourselves of how the Gospels came to be. When the Second Vatican Council wrote its document on Scripture, *Dei Verbum*, it noted the stages in what could be called the formation of the Gospel tradition. The first stage was the experience of Jesus of Nazareth, the lived experience of his followers. After his death and resurrection, there were the years of talking, remembering, sharing (rather than writing down the events) the memories of Jesus of Nazareth, but also the growing awareness of who he really was.

Jesus Christ Superstar reminds us that 'in 4 BC, there was no mass communication'. But now it might say that in early Christian times there was no social media – and we realise that even in the 21st century, accuracy is not the chief quality of social media.

Which means that the Jesus stories and memories – not photographic let alone instagrammatic – were inevitably not meant to be accurate versions. Each community shared the stories, thought about them in the light of the Jewish Scriptures, and emphasised how Jesus resembled/fulfilled those Scriptures, creative memories. Then, as the first disciples aged and died, it seemed time for the stories (and the reflections on conversations over the decades) to be written down, forming our four Gospels.

This background will come up in various chapters of this book, especially with some of the themes as we move from Gospel to Gospel.

There is also a focus on some images of Jesus, especially moving images from the many Jesus films. After all, in this social media century, where we read less and less, where we watch more and more, we have opportunities for the traditional *Lectio Divina*, Spiritual Reading, but now for *Visio Divina*, Spiritual Watching. The stories can come alive in our minds, imaginations and hearts as we read and as we see.

This is the emphasis in this book's subtitle. The Gospel reflections are to stimulate our minds and our understanding as well as to move our hearts and our emotions.

So, we can accompany Jesus again, in his ministry, in his revelation of what God is like in what Jesus said and what he did.

Jesus according to the Scriptures

You must keep to what you have been taught and know to be true: remember who your teachers were, and how, ever since you were a child, you have known the holy scriptures – from these you can learn the wisdom that leads to salvation through faith in Christ Jesus. All Scripture is inspired by God and can profitably be used for teaching, for refuting error, for guiding people's lives and teaching them to be holy. This is how all who are dedicated to God become fully equipped and ready for any good work.
(2 Timothy 3:14-17)

It seemed a good idea to quote this passage in full. It is not a text that everyone is familiar with, somewhat buried away in the second letter to Timothy and its final chapter. But for Gospel reflections for minds and hearts, it is key. I have found it the prayerful quotation to begin sessions for Gospel reflections.

It is the perspective from life in the early church – perhaps the next generation or so on from Jesus – preserving his memory, but also seeing him in the light of the heritage of the Hebrew Scriptures. In fact, this passage is referring to them. Which means that Jesus must be seen in the light of the Hebrew Scriptures, always.

And this is reinforced by an earlier text, from St Paul himself – Romans 15:4-6.

And indeed everything that was written long ago in the scriptures was meant to teach us something about hope from the examples scripture gives of how people who did not give up were helped by God.

Of course, Luke has Jesus himself reinforcing this perspective, even giving an 'Old Testament seminar' on the day of his resurrection, walking with those two doubting disciples to Emmaus, their not recognising him, his rebuking them, sad-faced, worried about their interpretation of who Jesus was, restorer of the kingdom of Israel. But he explained the inevitability, so to speak, of the death of the Christ, and took them through all the passages of the Scriptures that were about himself (Luke 24:27).

Decades ago, Catholics were not encouraged to read the Hebrew Scriptures. It would be interesting to go back and investigate why – perhaps they were read by Protestants and therefore not by Catholics, or that they were too difficult... But especially in the years following the end of World War II, there was a flourishing of Catholic scholarship, catching up with the already long-standing scholarship of Protestants from the 19th century, and the Catholic Church discovering the widest range of Scriptures, and the blessing of this loving appreciation from the decree of the Second Vatican Council, *Dei Verbum* (1965).

Which means that we become ever more sensitive to how the Hebrew Scriptures permeate the New Testament, permeate the Gospels.

On the one hand, there are the obvious explicit quotations, found in all the Gospels as well as in Acts and the range of epistles and the other books. Perhaps we have taken these for granted, even skimming over them. But we look at the infancy narratives in Matthew and realise how he uses them as fulfilment texts. Jesus is being paralleled with Moses in Egypt, for instance. We could list all the references to King David – quite a portrait of his hoped-for descendant, or the references to Jonah and intimations of resurrection.

On the other hand, a lot of the Hebrew Scripture references are more subtle, poetic, interwoven in the text. A quick example would be Luke's narrative of the Annunciation, rich in scriptural allusions – Gabriel the angelic announcer from the book of Daniel of the fullness of time (who had done the same thing announcing John to his father, Zechariah), allusions to mothers of saviours, back to King David and the oracles of the prophet Nathan, references to the Spirit, and the Isaian image of the maiden with child.

We can go to chapter 19 of John's Gospel, the chapter of the crucifixion of Jesus, the image of Jesus on the cross, thirsting, with his mother and beloved disciple, breathing forth his spirit, side pierced with the lance, references to blood and water, and references to Psalm texts and the prophet Zechariah. Over the centuries, painters have tried to incorporate these references in visual symbols.

In the last chapter of the Gospel of John (21:25), the author reminds his readers and listeners that there were many other things that Jesus said and did; 'If all were written down, the world itself, I suppose, would not hold all the books that would have to be written'. But the events in this Gospel have been recorded so that you may believe that Jesus is the Christ, the Son of God, and that believing this you may have life through his name.

This is something of what those words of the Nicene Creed indicate: Jesus according to the Scriptures...

Write your own Gospel

Somebody once asked me, 'What do you mean? We have Matthew, Mark, Luke, John. These are our Gospels'. And I added that there were also the many apocryphal Gospels from the early centuries of the church which continually turn up, promoted by enthusiasts over the years.

But that is not what I mean. Do you remember the story of *Fahrenheit 451*? That is Ray Bradbury's futuristic science-fiction parable where the firemen do not put out the fires; rather, they light them, especially burning books, Nazi fascist style. Culture to be eliminated. Rebels in the countryside memorise the text of books to preserve them. In the film version, someone was walking, reciting 'It was the best of times, it was the worst of times', Dickens and *A Tale of Two Cities*. I remember thinking at the time that there could have been someone reciting, 'In the beginning was the Word...', embodying John's Gospel.

In fact, for 'Write Your Own Gospel', I am indebted to a Jesuit (and, after St Ignatius, aren't we all!), Father John J. Navone, from the Gregorian University in Rome. In 1979, he wrote an article in *Review For Religious* on this theme. He suggested that a helpful exercise during a retreat might be to get a pad or an exercise book and write, from memory, one's own version of the Gospel stories, our own Gospel. And, in the past, some retreatants have done this, amazed at what they remember, but disappointed at what they don't remember, wondering about the accuracy of the memory, the priorities of the stories and passages they have written down.

So this is quite a prayerful challenge – not just going back into the memories of Gospel stories and texts that have accumulated over the years, but appreciating what surfaces in the memory, what are the stories that are most important to us, who is the Jesus that we remember, and who is alive in these Gospel memories.

Not everybody has the time and energy to write their own Gospel in full. So, over the years, I have suggested a particular approach. I would suggest we have seven chapters in our own Gospel, one from each of the key sections of the classic Gospels themselves. We could start with an Infancy story, then follow up with our favourite miracle story, an encounter that Jesus had which we like to dwell on, go back to. We should add a parable, a section of Jesus' teaching. And our own Gospel – like the classic four – would have a Passion story and a Resurrection story. Seven highlights for writing our own Gospel.

With an Infancy narrative, we have the choice between memories of Matthew and Luke, perhaps a focus on Bethlehem and the Magi, or stories of Nazareth from Luke. I have been constantly amazed at the range of miracle stories that people have chosen when they reflect on their Gospel, most people choosing a healing story, although a number have rather enjoyed sharing the marriage feast at Cana. As regards an encounter, I've been surprised to be reminded of characters who would not have been immediate choices for my own Gospel. But a great favourite has been Jesus meeting the woman at the well. And how is it, I wonder, that people have not chosen as their parable the Prodigal Son! Some have actually preferred the Sower and the Seed or the Labourers in the Vineyard!! And the Beatitudes often turn up as the choice for Jesus' teaching.

Over the years, one observation is that for the passion story, older people tend to choose Jesus and the Agony in the Garden whereas younger people tend to go to the Crucifixion. And I'm constantly amazed at the number of people who do not choose the Emmaus story as their Resurrection Gospel!

As you have been reading this, I hope that a whole number of stories are rising in your memory, that you appreciate that it is not too difficult at all to write your own Gospel. The challenge, in fact, is what to leave out rather than what to include.

The recommendation is that you take the opportunity to write it down, just in your own words (as if all the Gospels had disappeared like the scenario in *Fahrenheit 451*, no text for you to consult). What you write down may turn out to be a mixture or an amalgam of different pieces from different Gospels – but they are yours.

And if you don't have the opportunity to write your Gospel down but actually are part of a group doing this reflection together, it can be quite exhilarating to take some time to recollect and discover what stories surface, and then to share those experiences.

Many Christians in groups often find it difficult to share their faith but it is so much easier when talking about their Gospel choices. In fact, while I was working with a group of young pastoral workers, one girl shared her miracle story – the paralytic who was let down through the roof to Jesus' feet. The atmosphere of the session was momentarily shattered as another girl called out, highly enthusiastically, 'That was mine!'. And, of course, Catholics who are at home with charismatic renewal and sharing have no difficulty in communicating their story. (The facilitator often has to put a time limit!)

It is interesting to go back to 'Write Your Own Gospel' over the years to see whether our choices remain the same or new stories, new perspectives, on Jesus have opened up for us.

The Calling of Prophets

It seems a touch old-fashioned now to be referring to one's work or one's mission in life as a 'calling'. There is something rather dignified about it. A call to be a teacher, to be a doctor, to be an electrician, to be a sports coach... Worth checking to see whether people use this phrasing nowadays.

A calling is a vocation. Perhaps we use vocation less than calling. But in the good old days (were they?), especially in Catholic circles, vocation focused on the call to priesthood or religious life. By an extension (perhaps granted by the dominant celibates), vocation could also be used in reference to marriage.

Whatever the usage, one of the features of the Hebrew Scriptures is the focus on call, often dramatised literally, the call of the prophets. The emphasis, of course, is on God doing the calling, not the prophets setting themselves up as God's emissaries, speaking in the name of God, self-appointed Messiahs (as do some of the so-called prophets in recent times who have been unmasked). Then, aren't we all called to be prophets, each in our own way?

So, why not journey, briefly, through those stories of call and check with our own experiences?

The first prophet to experience a call offers the basic elements. It was Samuel, as a boy in the covenant shrine, hearing the voice of God during the night, thinking it was the priest, Eli, who wisely advised Samuel to respond, the response of each of us continuing in our own lives, 'Speak, Lord, your servant is listening'. Perfect.

But when it comes to what are called the classical prophets, there is quite a range of stories. The first of these prophets – whose oracles were different from the sagas told of Elijah and Elisha – was the unlikely countryman, Amos, out in the hills beyond Bethel, with the sheep and the sycamores. You have to delve into the book of Amos to pick out the call sequences. It is only in chapter 7, when he is severely criticised by the local priest, that Amos, quite definitely, declares that he is not one of the professional prophets around the city. Rather, he is out in the countryside, and has experienced God, compelling him to go into the town and speak out. (Glancing through some of the oracles, 'speaking out' seems something of an understatement in his denunciation of those who exploit the poor for a pair of sandals, who sit on their divans calling for another bowl of wine...!). Earlier in the book, Amos makes a list of rhetorical statements, stating the obvious about what one must do, culminating in 'the Lion roars: who can help feeling afraid? The Lord speaks: who can refuse to prophesy?'

His contemporary, Hosea, does not recount such a call but there is a narrative of his experience of seeking a wife, being sent to the pagan shrine in the hills to choose one of the shrine prostitutes, to marry her, to experience her infidelity, the challenge to his love, and, in the words of the hymn, 'Come back to me with all your heart...'.

But down in Jerusalem, there is a vivid description of a call, this time of the statesman, Isaiah, someone who had the ear of the king, but, experiencing God in the sanctuary, its shrine atmosphere, the incense, the ministering angels, the hot coal cauterising his tongue, God's request as to who will go and, 'Here I am, send me'.

The prophet Micah (6:8) summed up beautifully what God asks of us: 'to act justly, to love tenderly and to walk humbly with your God'.

During the time of what we might call the second Covenant Crisis, the invasion of the Babylonians, the siege of Jerusalem, the temple destroyed, the Ark of the Covenant lost, the people exiled, there were several key prophets. The call of Jeremiah was straightforward except that Jeremiah expressed his reluctance, excusing himself that he was only young – irritating God, so to speak, who said that he was putting his words on Jeremiah's mouth and that he must go and preach. Ezekiel, on the other hand, a man of symbols and images, saw a spectacular vision of God – fire, wheels, faces of ox, lion, eagle, a man, and taking God's scroll, eating God's Word – and it tasted like honey.

Perhaps we are more like Jeremiah than Ezekiel!

But the prophet who may be dear to our hearts, whose story is recounted in the liturgies of Holy Week, is the anonymous man who was referred to as God's servant, and whom we call the suffering servant. In the first song, his call is quiet, beloved by God, delighting God, specially chosen, whose mission is to bring justice, not by crying out, not by domination. This call is reinforced in the second song, a sense of mission, and, in time of difficulty, the servant committing his cause unreservedly to God.

And then things change. The third song opens with awakening with delight, but then comes the hostility, the spit, the slap, beard being pulled... Which leads to the climax in the fourth song, a high point in the Hebrew Scriptures, where the servant suffers, quietly, the Lamb victim led to the slaughter, but for us, all the time bearing our sins, and yet, in hope of rising again, new life.

What a heritage for us in our reflection on vocation, on the experience of call. And, then, Jesus was to come.

Spirituality of
Apostles, Evangelisers

We are all called to evangelise, each of us in our own way. In whatever life we are called to, we are apostles. In a reading of the Gospels, Jesus and his choice of twelve apostles offers us some perspectives on a missionary spirituality.

In *Jesus Christ Superstar*, after the episode of the Last Supper, while Jesus realises he is about to go into agony, the apostles wander off drowsily to sleep, singing the amusingly ironic lyrics:

> Always hoped that I'd be an apostle.
> Knew that I would make it if I tried.
> Then when we retire, we can write the Gospels,
> So they'll still talk about us when we've died.

Of course, we know that it was not like this at all. The Twelve were very ordinary men. Matthew was probably the most qualified and educated as a tax collector. Judas must have had abilities for his role with the finances. Peter, Andrew, James and John fished for a living. Then there is doubting Thomas, Philip brought into the action once or twice, the call of Nathaniel, Simon named as a Zealot, nothing really about James or Jude. And yet, Jesus spent the night in prayer, gathered his disciples, chose and named these Twelve, representing the Twelve tribes of Israel.

As we look at the list of the Twelve, we realise that some were headliners, had starring roles so to speak. Others were in the supporting cast. Some had particular cameos. Others seem to be extras, in the crowd.

So what do the experiences of the apostles offer us? First of all, there is the experience of call, the Twelve together, but Jesus meeting Simon Peter, giving him the name of Cephas, Rock. The fishermen are at their work then leave their nets to follow Jesus. It seems that the first quality in the spirituality of an apostle is the surrender to the call, acknowledging its absolute, to leave everything aside for that call.

Peter's experience serves as something of a model for those who are called to evangelise in an up-front way, leadership. It is he who speaks, inspired by grace, on behalf of the others, recognising who Jesus is, given a commission as Rock. But his path is in fact a rocky road, impetuous, presumptuous, offering to shield Jesus from suffering but told that he is a Satan, a stumbling block, and to get behind him. He is the same at that marvellous moment when Jesus offers the new covenant law of love, washing the apostles' feet, Peter refusing and then, extreme, wanting to be washed all over. Bravado in Gethsemane, denial when challenged by servants, disappearance during the crucifixion. But offered the chance for rehabilitation, his declaration of love, affirmation of his commission of leadership and evangelisation, 'Feed, lovingly tend, my sheep'.

There is also the spirituality of the prominent trio, Peter, James and John, privileged to be taken aside by Jesus, experiencing the wonder of a transfiguring vision of who Jesus really is, especially present when Jesus raises the little girl to life – but not enough to sustain them and keep them awake in Gethsemane.

Scholars raise the difficulty of the Beloved Disciple named in John's Gospel, whether he is John himself or another disciple, the one who knew the high priest and could get into Jesus' trial, who stood at the foot of the cross, comforting Mary, his being entrusted to her, and she to him. And that intimation at the end of John's Gospel when Peter asked what would happen to him, Jesus told Peter not to be concerned whether the disciple might live longer...

It looks as though the spirituality of an apostle has heights, has depths, sometimes profound, often particularly mundane.

Matthew is, ultimately, a success story – starting in a sinful, early exploitative career, conversion, named for a Gospel. Thomas, on the other hand, offers a pattern for many an apostle – born sceptic, so to speak, then willing to go to Jerusalem to suffer with Jesus, curious of mind and asking questions after the Last Supper (and Jesus revealing to Thomas and the others that he is the way, the truth and the life) and then the high drama after the resurrection, hypersceptical, doubting the resurrection, not believing the testimony of the others, the demand to touch the wounds – and the rapid capitulation, 'My Lord and My God'.

Nathaniel represents the hesitater, the questioner, but the one who is overwhelmed by the encounter with Jesus himself. Philip, on the other hand, is the facilitator, helping out when the followers of Jesus were hungry in the desert, introducing Greeks to Jesus, asking questions during Jesus' discourse after the Last Supper. Many of us could respond to the patterns of Nathaniel moving to enthusiasm, Philip happy in welcoming and supporting roles.

The others are those anonymous evangelisers, perhaps in a less obvious world, images of yeast rising in the dough coming to mind...

But at the time of crisis, the apostles fail, hiding away in the upper room. But they have been called; and Jesus cannot let them down. He comes, he reassures them, sees them fishing, he eats, blesses them as he leaves and exhorts them to go out to all the nations. And this exhortation and promise is fulfilled, the Spirit coming at Pentecost, the extraordinary transformation, their going out courageously, so many exciting stories in the Acts of the Apostles, preaching, healing, creating community, travelling, martyred.

And yet, who is the apostle of the resurrection? The woman who has joined the group who follow Jesus in his ministry and care for him. Mary Magdalene, who was at the foot of the cross, who came to the tomb early in the morning, met Jesus without recognising him, was overjoyed at his revelation, was commissioned to go back to the Twelve, to Peter himself, to announce the resurrection to him. So... over to us to reflect on the pattern of the apostle as embodied in Mary Magdalene.

And then, to Paul, called an Apostle, the next generation.

Jesus and his Encounters

During workshops on the theme of 'Write Your Own Gospel', I am always eager to hear the sharing of the choices, the favourites, about Jesus and an encounter, not a miracle, just Jesus meeting people. And I always expect – and the expectation is fulfilled – that a number of people will choose one story over and above others. And that is the story from John 4 – the woman at the well. It is also one of the longest chapters in all the Gospels.

And in thinking about other Gospel encounters, it is women who come to the fore. There is the woman who gatecrashes Simon the Pharisee's dinner, labelled in some translations as the woman who was a sinner in the city (Luke 7). And, on that same theme, we go to John 8, Jesus' encounter with the woman taken in adultery.

The three women in these encounters were known, shamed and vilified in public. Jesus did not shame them. But he certainly raised the eyebrows of those who condemned the women, indicating some disapproval of their judgment or harshness, challenging them for their lack of compassion. In fact, this did not always work. When the woman at the well – who had an opportunity to have a long conversation with Jesus, enabling her to confront what was happening in her life, to be embarrassed, but to be reassured and encouraged – she is the one to whom Jesus promised, as he does to all of us, the gift of living water. And in the middle of this, the disciples return with news about where to eat and react rather censoriously to Jesus talking with the woman. She was deeply moved by this encounter with Jesus, appreciation from this unexpected man who engaged in conversation, requesting a drink. When she went to tell everybody about her experience, the townspeople fobbed her off, dismissing her because they had experienced Jesus for themselves.

The prostitute in Luke 7 had been so moved by Jesus and rushed, definitely uninvited, into Simon the Pharisee's dinner, knowing the qualities of the man she was approaching. She expected forgiveness. And so, with symbols and symbolic action, she wept, brushing Jesus' wet feet with her hair, and anointing them with ointment. Simon and his guests were not the least bit impressed, insinuating that Jesus could not discern the quality of people, that any respectable person would not even respond to this woman. If you have never seen this episode in Franco Zeffirelli's *Jesus of Nazareth*, I would highly recommend it. It is preceded by the Pharisees' discussion with Jesus about his tolerance and not judging, about the law of love of neighbour, and the question: Who is my neighbour?.

Then Anne Bancroft appears, the woman weeping and anointing. But the camera focuses on Robert Powell as Jesus, his quiet reaction, his being moved, his halting the interjection of Simon, his praise of the woman, beloved and forgiven. Many of the guests were not the least bit persuaded, indicating that they thought Jesus' comments were blasphemous, that it was only God who can forgive sins. Or perhaps some of them were moved, admiring Jesus and his forgiveness, discovering the compassion of God in Jesus.

It was far less easy for the woman taken in adultery, dragged before Jesus, denounced, the authorities setting up a trap for Jesus to condemn himself. We have often re-lived the story as we have listened, or seen it depicted in films, the writing in the sand, the embarrassment of those condemning the woman, certainly no one owning up to be innocent and so eligible to cast the first stone, their slinking away. And Jesus, left with the woman, raising her up, freeing her, enabling her to sin no more.

Jesus' encounter with a male character is harder to come by. The main candidate is the tax collector, Zacchaeus. But some commentators note that this is a male variation on the story of the woman taken in adultery. There are some nice story touches: Zacchaeus is short, is curious to see Jesus, climbs a tree, literally goes out on a limb, branches out, so to speak, even turning a new leaf! But Jesus reaches out and up. Once again, there is the imagery of eating and drinking, Jesus choosing to dine with this financial reprobate who is touched, repents in his own way and offers restitution, more even than justice might demand.

Isn't it interesting that in the early church, in those early communities who were sharing their memories of Jesus, listening to the stories of the witnesses, that in the key stories of encounters, it was sinful people who were attracted to him? – and, we might say, brought out the best in him.

Jesus' Friends

We sometimes say we can learn a lot about a person when we consider their friends. We can ask the same about Jesus' friends. This is Jesus social and sociable.

In looking at the Gospels, we find that the household in Bethany was a place where Jesus could really feel at home. It was the home of Martha, Mary and Lazarus. We see Jesus at his most relaxed. But we will come back to that.

In the meantime, we can look at other passages to find out how Jesus was, what he was like, when he was with those he liked so much.

Early in Matthew's Gospel, there is an incident where Jesus seems to be very much at home in Peter's household. There seems to be some trouble because Peter's mother-in-law is ill. And Jesus heals her, with the added detail that she got up and provided hospitality for her guests. And, speaking of hospitality, Luke does mention the group of women, some of whom had experience of evil spirits and ailments, Mary Magdalene (the emphasis is on her sickness of seven evil spirits, no condemnation of her behaviour), Joanna, wife of Herod's steward, Susannah, Mary, who went around the countryside ministering to the apostles from their own resources (Luke 8:1-3). And in this context of Jesus' friendly outreach to women, we remember his consoling words to the women so distressed at watching him carrying his cross to Calvary.

Which means, then, that we should look for an example of male friend over and above the apostles. While the narrative is not exactly a story of friendship, Jesus' meeting with the Pharisee, Nicodemus, gets a great deal of attention in the Gospel of John. For one thing, it is not initially a public friendship. Nicodemus, apprehensive but curious, visits Jesus under cover of night for some serious discussions. The friendship begins with intellectual concerns, theological concerns. But Jesus takes the opportunity to reveal something of the mysteries of God, God's love in the incarnation, to this questing Pharisee. And, of course, at the end, along with Joseph of Arimathea, it is Nicodemus who approaches Pontius Pilate as well as providing for the burial of Jesus.

In Zeffirelli's *Jesus of Nazareth*, as Jesus carries his cross, there is a voice-over reciting, so aptly, the fourth Servant Song. The fine voice is that of Laurence Olivier. And who does Olivier portray in the series? Nicodemus.

But the most telling portrait of Jesus as friend is his love for Martha, Mary and Lazarus. There is something very homely in the telling of the story. Those of us who are prone to be busy, busy, have a certain feel for Martha as she prepares the meal, upset that her sister is absenting herself, sitting like an attentive disciple at Jesus' feet. Jesus, the friend, is able to pacify Martha in some ways, urging her not to 'worry and fret about so many things'. Jesus does commend Mary for her careful listening, 'the better part'. In fact, the next passage in Luke's Gospel is on Martha's side – the Good Samaritan, and the urging of disciples to listen to God but to go in action, even action beyond the call of duty. These two stories provide a balance between contemplation and action.

It is not reported, unfortunately perhaps, that Jesus and the apostles helped with clearing the tables and wiping up.

But the story of Jesus' friendship with the family is narrated in one of the most powerful stories in John (chapter 11). Lazarus is ill. The sisters send a message to Jesus but he seems to dillydally and not hurry to Lazarus' bedside. He does tell the apostles – especially the upset Thomas (ready to accompany him and die) – that there is a reason for what he does and does not do. And when he does arrive, Lazarus already four days in the tomb, the two sisters act in the way that we might expect. Martha, active, hurries out to meet Jesus, regretting his delay, if only... On the other hand, Mary sits in her grief. The death of Lazarus provides the opportunity for one of those Signs and Wonders that feature in John's Gospel, Jesus calling to Lazarus, bringing him out of the tomb, taking away the winding cloths, Lazarus alive.

One of the great features of this narrative is what has happened to Martha, from her being busy at the meal in Bethany to her being the person who first hears one of Jesus' greatest revelations. It is to Martha that he tells that he is the resurrection and the life. Martha has certainly gone on a faith journey.

And then in chapter 12, there is once again hospitality and a meal, many of the curious from Jerusalem coming out to see the resuscitated Lazarus. And the pattern occurs again. Martha is serving everyone at the table, her forte (but not worrying and fretting). And it is Mary who then contemplatively anoints Jesus – as he says, in anticipation of his death and burial.

Jesus was comfortable with Martha, Mary and Lazarus. How comfortable are we in appreciating the friendliness of Jesus?

Jesus Heals

Miracles are a major feature of the Gospels. When John the Baptist sends messengers to Jesus to ask about him, Jesus quotes the book of Isaiah: the blind see again, the lame walk, lepers are cleansed, the deaf hear, the dead are raised to life... (Luke 7:22). Miracles are a sign of God's healing Covenant presence and intervention in our world. And, in John's Gospel, they are Signs and Wonders.

A very good lesson I learned about Jesus and miracles came from a Methodist minister, working with indigenous people in the Northern Territory. He was critical of some government interventions, decisions by government about what was good for Aboriginal people and giving it to them – whether they wanted it or not! He quoted the encounter between Jesus and the blind man, Bartimaeus. He pointed out that Jesus did not rush in to restore the man's sight by zapping him. Rather, he asked, 'What would you have me do for you?' Jesus was a respecter of people, their hopes and desires, not a compulsive or compulsory do-gooder.

We can take a number of popular miracle stories and reflect on what they reveal about Jesus, his concern for people, miracles as an outpouring of his love, but meeting people at the level of their own experience.

Walking around with his disciples, he comes across a funeral procession and is moved by what he sees, going up to comfort a bereft mother, a widow, sharing her pain, putting his hand on the bier, breathing new life into her son – 'and Jesus gave him to his mother'. And, when he went to the tomb of Lazarus, Jesus is so moved and there is one of the briefest of gospel verses, 'Jesus wept'.

Sometimes Jesus is taken by surprise. He is on his way, at the request of Jairus whose daughter is dying. But he is interrupted, something physically and emotionally happening to him. The woman suffering the haemorrhage has come up behind him, touched the hem of his cloak, hoping to be healed. Jesus realises that power has gone out of him. And it has healed the woman, fearful, but he then reassures her. We realise that in his healing self-giving, it does take something out of him, the healings can be draining experiences. Healings can be strange experiences in this way – his spitting and making a paste for a ritual healing of the deaf man.

Then there is the eager Jesus, hurrying to Jairus' house only to find the little girl dead – becoming rather short with the mourners, ousting them for their professional weeping and lamenting then quietly and privately taking the little girl's hand and raising her to life – and urging 'give her something to eat'. At another time, when the Roman centurion came to make a request that Jesus cure his servant, he is eager to go but in the famous words, immortalised in the celebration of the Eucharist and Communion, the centurion – his faith astounding Jesus – declares there is no need for Jesus to come to his house but only say the word and his servant would be healed.

There were some dramatic healings: roof tiles suddenly removed and a paralytic man on a stretcher lowered down in front of Jesus. There are some disappointments as well: Jesus healing ten lepers but only one coming back to express some gratitude (and he was a despised foreigner, a Samaritan).

One of the most dramatic healings stories – and one of the longest – is John's story of the man born blind (chapter 9). It is not just a miracle story. There is a faith setting, a questioning of the theology of inherited blame, a sharing of parental guilt, with the issue of whether the man was blind because he was a sinner or was it because of his ancestors (actually, the prophet Ezekiel had criticised this blame-theology three times in his prophecies, more than 500 years before the coming of Jesus).

The chapter is written like a drama (and could work very effectively in liturgy when it occurs in Lent with a variety of voices taking part: Jesus, the disciples, the Pharisees, the blind man's parents, and the blind man himself with his smart answer to the Pharisees scoffing at them that they might want to become disciples!). The dramatic highlight is that the man did not recognise who it was that healed him and the denouement, so to speak, is Jesus quietly encountering the man in the temple and their personal discussion about what this meant for him and his future.

You may like all these miracle stories but there may be others that you particularly value, that you cherish. Who is the Jesus that is revealed in your favourite miracle stories?

A Perspective on Discipleship

Probably our first thought when discipleship is mentioned is Jesus' statement that if anyone wants to be his disciple, they must take up their cross and follow him. This discipleship is a laying down of life in order to gain it. Dietrich Bonhoeffer famously referred to 'The Cost of Discipleship' – and, in Nazi Germany, the cost was his life.

It is an understatement to say that Jesus' chosen Twelve were not always quick on the uptake, not understanding what their call to discipleship entailed. We might remember that intrusion of mother-love, mother-preferment, when the mother of the sons of Zebedee, James and John, was caught up with ambition. She had confidence in her approach to Jesus, used the language of the coming reign of God, not just making the request, but actually demanding a promise from Jesus that when the reign came, her two sons would sit on each side of Jesus. Jesus was compelled to say that she did not know what she was asking. And he challenged the two sons whether they were willing to share his sufferings and endure with him. They asserted that they were. But Jesus reminded them that whatever happened, it would be the choice of God, his father.

Which means, then, that there is always an inherent danger of being presumptuous, even in discipleship.

And that leads to one of the key passages about discipleship in Matthew 20:20-23. On listening in to the mother-request, the other ten murmur, growl, become indignant. But this leads to one of the great expressions about discipleship. Jesus declares that it is a 'pagan', non-believing, self-centred, thing to lord it over others. That kind of authority enjoys making its power felt. And Jesus declares, emphatically, 'This is not to happen among you'. And he offers the key to discipleship – if you want to be great, you must be a servant; if you want to be first, you must be a slave. And the profound rationale, motivation – just as the Son of Man came, not to be served, but to serve, and to give his life as a ransom.

Some kind of awareness and training in being this kind of servant should be on the CV of every disciple.

One of the best elaborations of what this kind of servant-service should be can be found expressed in Philippians 2:1-5. St Paul, towards the end of his life, after travels and complicated mission experiences and encounters, urges the Philippians, 'In your minds, you must be the same as Christ Jesus'. I always like to add: In your minds *and in your hearts*, you must be the same as Christ Jesus. He then quotes what may have been a popular hymn in the communities at that time, the wonder that Jesus whom they confessed 'in the form of God' would empty himself, living like us; and astonishment that Jesus should accept death, death on a cross. Jesus bears the complete cost of discipleship – but is raised to new life. The reward of discipleship.

I would like to add to these perspectives on discipleship another passage, Matthew 11:25-30. Jesus is in an exhilarated frame of mind and heart, rejoicing that those who follow him have had truth revealed to them, whether they were clever or not. It is a gift. And in that light, he speaks of his reward for discipleship, responding to his invitation to come to him, especially those who labour and are overburdened. Jesus gives rest. And he reminds his listeners that there is still disciple's work to be done, and he is the model for it, shouldering a yoke like the cattle that could be seen in the fields, bound together by the yoke, working and pulling together, going in the same direction, energy not scattered. And this can bring the reward of rest for discipleship and the discovery that Jesus' yoke is easy, his burden light.

The cross, real or figurative, is the yoke that has to be borne But, ultimately, cross-bearing in faith can be light.

Jesus and a Justice Charter

At any era of world history, but particularly in our own times, we have a need for Gospel insights into justice. Where did Jesus stand on justice issues?

The Hebrew people had their Covenant Justice Charter with the Ten Commandments. And, for Jesus and his contemporaries, they were still living that charter. However, with his emphasis on the new law of love, the new Covenant Love, he provided a further charter: the Beatitudes.

The heart of the Beatitudes is found in the first, the naming of the poor in heart, the *anawim*, the Hebrew word for the people of the earth, the grounded people, feet on the ground. (A glance back at the prophet Zephaniah reveals praising comments on these 'poor in spirit' people – and the prophet Amos, particularly, is grieved at how they were treated by the wealthy who had a poverty of humanity.)

I'm sure we have all been taken through the Beatitudes many a time to highlight the qualities Jesus presents and the happy and blessed consequences of living those qualities. The merciful will be shown mercy – a fundamental justice principle and those grieving and mourning will be comforted. The pure in heart, those with the best of intentions, will see God. The meek, those who are not pushy and dominating that is, will find their place on this earth. Of course, peacemaking is an obvious justice principle. Justice is spelt out with those who hunger and thirst for what is right and the promise that they will be satisfied. But discipleship has a cost, and so there are those who are persecuted in the cause of right – maybe not being rewarded here on earth, but the promise that God is with them.

We live in an age (probably true of every age) with huge gaps between the rich and the poor. Jesus reminds his followers that we cannot be servants both of God and of money. And money (sometimes with the addition of 'that tainted thing') is the cause of so much trouble, and the desire for money the root of all evil. Look at the parable of the rich man and Lazarus, luxury in this life, hellish deprivations in the next. And, by contrast, the parable of the labourers in the vineyard where a just wage is paid by the landowner not confined by strict conditions in contracts, happy to give a bonus at the end of the day. Jesus also tells parables of responsible management, the entrusting of the talents, for people to do their best with what they have. Jesus, in his ironic moments, also has the satire of the conniving servant who is sacked, who gets into the accounts, alters the amount of debt owed, excels in mismanagement to make his future life comfortable, 'Dig I am not able, beg I am ashamed'. Jesus comments on the fraud skills of the servant but his point is... Not.

And peace and war? Mediation is necessary – but Jesus offers an exhortation that those quarrelling make peace along the way, before arbitration.

And in a church and world where Pope Francis – in *Laudato Si'* – has solemnly alerted us to the dangers to the environment, to the fostering of the wonders of creation of which St Francis of Assisi sang, we recall Jesus, at a poetic moment in the Sermon on the Mount, enthusing about the birds of the air, the flowers of the field, the providence of God that sustains them, and how the same God's Providence will sustain us.

Jesus' Story of the (Most) Permissive Father

You may well be ahead of me as you read the title. Yes, the reference is to what is traditionally known as the parable of the Prodigal Son, sometimes referred to as the Prodigal Father. However, I rather like describing the father of the parable as permissive, most permissive.

If we want to know what God is like, what God our Father is like, it is revealed to us in what Jesus said and did. In speaking this parable, Jesus enables us to appreciate a great deal about God. He is talking about his own Father.

Who, in any serious family situation, would tolerate an upstart son, trying to assert some autonomy, motivated by self-interest, by the prospect of easy money, by horizons of no supervision and no restraints? Hard to know what Jesus' initial listeners were making of this. After all, they had the models of patriarchal fathers, of the norms for the ideal father from the Wisdom literature, teaching and instructing their sons in the ways of the law and of God.

But in one swoop, credibility is tested. The father does not hesitate in granting his son's wishes. Is he not the most permissive father? And as a consequence – I more than suppose – we have to ask what this means in terms of the permissiveness of God, giving us our free will, allowing us to do what we choose, what we decide, no matter whether it is offensive to God or destructive for others. No matter what the consequences – and they are eventually dire for the wastrel son.

All goes exhilaratingly at first, no limit to the cash flow, ready availability of what the son desires (and, in some translations, doesn't the older son – subconsciously envious – talk with disdain about his brother's sexual behaviour, 'he and his women'?). Then the unpredictable, the unhoped for, the drastically unexpected. Famine, no money, menial jobs, even prepared to eat pigs' slop to survive (and the thought comes that Jesus was indulging in unnecessary offensive detail for his Pharisee audience, not the eating of unclean pork, but the desperation of longing to survive on the sty's discarded garbage).

But Jesus wants to continue the story of the permissive father who becomes a forgiving father. Because he had let his son go, not lectured or reprimanded him, the son did not feel that he had been discarded, is able to come to his senses, discover emotions of repentance, affirm amendment of life in coming to his father, admitting what he had done, sorry for the offence, prepared to take his place as a servant to survive.

And the father? Jesus tells us that the father was an on-the-lookout kind of father, always hoping, eager that his son would return. And, when he sees him, does he stand, perhaps arms folded, noting how long it would take the son to reach him after he hoves in sight? No, the on-the-lookout father is a run-to-meet-him permissive father, eager for any initial sign of sorrow, change of heart. And when he runs to the son, he doesn't cut off the son's need for vocalising his sorrow. He hears out his act of contrition, so to speak.

Then, no holds barred, a kiss, an embrace, lavish joy, best robe, sandals, nothing is too good for a penitent and reconciling son. And kill the fatted calf! The father being enthusiastically permissive, feast, celebration for all. The son was lost. He is found.

And while this is the main focus of the story and why we enjoy it so much, there is still the third act, so to speak. That older son. To begin with, we didn't hear his views on his brother's behaviour but certainly now we know. This is the indignation of the righteous (self-righteous). Complaining about his constant fidelity to his father, obedience, hard work, surfacing an up-till-now resentment against brother and father. He won't go in, is not that kind of person (no wonder he complains of his father not giving him an animal for a feast for him and his friends – and perhaps we are surprised to find that he has friends!). And the rashest character in Jesus' parables – the servant who quickly blabs to the older son all that is happening.

What is a permissive father to do in the face of the anger of someone who would claim not to be a sinner in any way, has always done the right thing, but who finds himself in a moral crisis? The on-the-lookout father also goes out to meet this son, listening patiently to his complaint (including that Freudian allusion to the women and his brother). The permissive father tries to explain the situation of the younger brother, lost and found, a cause for joy. And then, in brief, most beautiful words, Godly words to the older son, and to us who listen to the parable: 'You are with me always and all I have is yours'. Including the father's all-encompassing love.

Many of those listening to Jesus' words were scribes and Pharisees, complaining about sinners coming to Jesus and his having a meal with them. They now have their answer. This is exactly what God is like.

Jesus: Man with no Name

There is a reason for me to call Jesus the man with no name. However, we do know that, even before his birth, his name was announced: Jesus, the saviour. And he answered to that all the way through his life – and we remember in the garden of Gethsemane, the soldiers approaching and Jesus asking whom they sought: Jesus of Nazareth. I am he.

And then we remember that when the Pharisees asked Jesus his name, especially his coming from Nazareth, they looked down their noses, so to speak or literally, and asked whether anything good could come from Nazareth! In other Gospels, there was acknowledgment of Nazareth, but all that the neighbours could come up with at that time was a condescending statement remembering that he was the carpenter's son.

However, there were times when he was not known, when he did ask his disciples questions about his name.

But the reason for the heading of this chapter comes from a reading of one of Jesus' first miracles, in the first chapter of Mark's Gospel, the story of the leper who came to Jesus and asked him to heal him. For most of us, it never occurs just how scandalous a story this is! When we read Leviticus and the dire rules and regulations for those who had contracted a disease like leprosy, we know that the leper had no business coming so near to Jesus. Like some of the blind beggars in other Gospel passages, he could simply have called out, drawing Jesus' attention to him and making his request.

So we realise – whether everyone knew Jesus' name or not – he was very approachable, but in health terms, dangerously so. And then, do we remember what Jesus did? He touched the sick man. Some of us are suspicious of the touchy-feely! But in many a Gospel story, that is really a fine and accurate description of Jesus. The translation in Mark has Jesus replying, 'Of course, I want to'.

Then – something of a surprise – the Jesus who has been somewhat oblivious of the laws of isolation suddenly becomes highly official, quoting the law in some detail and issuing a command to the man he has just healed. The leper is to present himself to the priest for verification and a certificate of health... and tell no one. If we had been healed of leprosy like this, we would have been shouting our enthusiasm to all and sundry and beyond. Which is what the leper did.

And Jesus remained outside the towns and villages. It was only later, during a retreat, listening to the leader verbally reflect on Gospel stories as we watched slides from Zeffirelli's *Jesus of Nazareth*, that the realisation came... that Jesus had become the leper! He had to go into isolation according to the law. He had to live in quarantine (not in Covid 19 hotel comfort/or lack of it) but on the outer, and, not only that, he had to rip his clothes, rub himself with dirt, and – the final humiliation – not able to name himself. Instead, like the other lepers, his name is a no-name, 'Unclean'. So, Jesus experienced anonymity, deprived of his name, forced to publicly identify himself by his unhealthy condition.

Yet, on the other hand, there are some passages where Jesus is quite insistent on his name. In the middle of Matthew's Gospel, Jesus actually asks the disciples what people were saying about him, who they thought he was. Some superstitious answers are offered, including Elijah or one of the prophets come back to life. But the wonderful point is that it is Peter, the rock who was to be the foundation of his followers, who has a grace-inspired moment, acknowledging Jesus as the Son of God.

Jesus' name was important at the end of his life. In the interrogations in his trials before Annas and Caiaphas, Jesus was challenged as to his identity. At this moment – more self-revelation – he identified himself with a figure from the Hebrew Scriptures, the Son of Man (from Daniel, chapter 7), coming on the clouds of heaven into the presence of God, bringing those who are faithful with him into the heavenly court. Verdict: blasphemy.

An ironic variation on Jesus having a name or not is the story of Pilate writing the inscription, King of the Jews, and the political and religious quibble by the authorities that Pilate should write that he said he was King of the Jews. Pilate had had enough. 'What I have written, I have written.' And this inscription is seen still in some crucifixion images.

But St Paul has a glorious, final word about Jesus' name. As Jesus was on the cross breathing forth his spirit, it was as if that spirit was his 'yes' to his father, the complete yes, and we can imagine God reaching out from the heavens, embracing the dead Jesus into new and risen life. (I am indebted to my friend, Michael Fallon MSC, for this image.) And so, in Philippians 2, the hymn St Paul quotes reminds us that not only did Jesus empty himself, taking human form, like ours, even to death – but God raised him and gave him a name that is above all names and that everyone, below the earth, on the earth, above the earth, must confess that Jesus is Lord.

From no name to the greatest name.

The New and Everlasting Covenant

Those, of course, are the words from the Eucharistic prayer, the Institution narrative. It is well worthwhile to look at their meaning.

For the old Covenant, we go back to the book of Exodus in chapters 19, 20 and 24. Chapter 19 has the people of Israel, having escaped through the Red Sea, arriving at Mount Sinai, their leader, Moses, going up to the mountain (where earth meets sky, image of where the human touches the divine) and experiencing the extraordinary initiative of the God of Abraham, Isaac and Jacob, the living God that Moses encountered at the burning bush, who revealed himself as the living God.

The extraordinary aspect of the old Covenant is that not only did God reach out to the people, whether they appreciated it or not, pledging a divine promise for constant fidelity, justice, lovingkindness (*hesed*) no matter what, no matter whether the people turned away, denied the Covenant. The pledge of God is to reach out – always. That is the kind of God they discovered.

But, of course, this Covenant agreement is to be lived out day-by-day. And so, we find Exodus 20 and the law by which the Covenant can be lived, the Ten Commandments. These commandments are not like so many of the other pieces of legislation elaborated in other chapters of Exodus and Leviticus. The description of those other pieces of legalisation is 'casuistic': case law, depending on situations, circumstances and applications. The Ten Commandments, on the other hand, are very direct, pointing out what should be done and what should not be done. Of course, there are nuances, but the Ten Commandments highlight the areas of moral living in principle.

The Hebrew people were the chosen of God, and the Covenant had to be ratified, religiously. In Exodus 24, the people are assembled at the foot of Mount Sinai, an altar set up, Aaron and the priests on one side, the people on the other, 12 sacred stones in front of them, symbolising the 12 tribes of Israel. According to the ritual of those times, animal victims are chosen, some absolutely consumed by fire, a sacrifice, called a Holocaust. Other animals are cooked, shared amongst the people, food in communion. The lifeblood of the animals is sprinkled on the altar, representing God, as well as sprinkled on the stones, representing the people, the union in the blood of the sacrifice, the people believing that life was in the blood.

This is the background for the new and everlasting Covenant.

The Gospels highlight Jesus and the apostles at the Last Supper (later understandings, disputed as always, suggest that other disciples, including women, might have been present as they were later in the upper room, gathered in prayer before the coming of the Spirit).

Jesus is the new Covenant. Jesus is God's outreach, the divine initiative of love for God's people. He is the pledge of constant fidelity, justice, complete love. And with the very nature of God becoming human, Jesus living our life with us, he is also the mediator of the Covenant.

And the new law? That is a highlight of John's account of the Last Supper (that Gospel leaving reflections on Eucharist and the Bread of Life to elaboration in chapter 6). In John 13, Jesus performs a prophetic symbolic action (as so many of the classical prophets did in the past). He does something that everybody could see, that everybody could remember and appreciate. Jesus, the Master, takes the role of the servant, a towel around his waist, kneeling, the basin of water, washing the feet of his apostles. And then, verbalising the point, that just as he had washed their feet, they were to wash others' feet.

And highlighting this symbol, he announces that he is giving them a new commandment, the new commandment of the new Covenant, not abolishing the Ten Commandments, but rather the deeper reality that underlies the whole human experience, the whole of human morality, profound love. What kind of love? 'Love one another as I have loved you.' There is no greater love, like Jesus laying down his life for his friends, and not just in culminating death, but in day-by-day ordinary living and interactions.

Which means, then, that the new, everlasting Covenant is ratified in Jesus' passion and death. Tradition has talked about Jesus as the victim, the altar, the priest. He is the Lamb of God led to the slaughter bearing our sins for us but this is anticipated ritually at the Last Supper, another prophetic symbolic action, when Jesus holds some bread and states, this is me – and shares it in communion. He holds up the cup of wine and states, this is me – and shares it in communion.

And Jesus exhorts us that we do this in memory of him: whenever we eat this bread and drink this cup, we proclaim his death and all that it means until he comes again.

The new Covenant is everlasting.

Speaking of Jesus' Resurrection

Speaking – and writing – of Jesus' resurrection was a more challenging task for the early Christian communities than we might think.

Years were passing. The disciples who knew and walked with Jesus were growing older, dying. The local communities had their particular memories which they continued to recount, mull over, being formed into received accounts that they passed on. They did this with all the events of Jesus' life – the Gospel period when Jesus was with them. But as Luke, for instance, discusses at the beginning of his Gospel as well as for the Acts of the Apostles, there was a certain shaping of the stories, the events, a timeline, with Luke using some Greek-Roman traditions in composing the portrait of a hero. The Matthew community, on the other hand, tended to focus on the teaching of Jesus, his great sermons, which form the core of the Gospel. John, of course, was written some decades after the other Gospels, with an extended time and experience to choose which events to write about, how to write them.

The events of Jesus of Nazareth and his ministry have prologues that set a tone to each Gospel. Mark quotes a passage from the second Isaiah heralding the coming of the expected Messiah. John has the hymn of the Word and the Incarnation. Matthew and Luke have what are called 'the infancy narratives'. The infancy narratives are stories: Matthew's carefully shaped as fulfilment of Old Testament prophecies, Luke's a more accessible story of incarnation, birth, life at Nazareth, Mary and Joseph tested in the Temple. Some commentators have referred to this as 'beginning language'.

I once had the joy of listening to an American Franciscan theologian, Kenan Osborne, who took up this theme but especially concerning the narratives of Jesus' resurrection. He referred to these as 'end language'. There were no precedents for writing about someone who had died, who was risen, was alive. There was only the ordinary language we have to describe ordinary events, so to speak. Kenan Osborne suggests we be attentive to what the different Gospels are doing to try to communicate that the Jesus of Nazareth whom they had known was now different and yet the same.

We could ask what our favourite resurrection story is. Are we with Mary Magdalene searching in the garden and Jesus revealing himself? Peter and John running to the empty tomb? Jesus appearing first in the upper room? The drama of the Thomas aftermath the week later? Speaking of memories, a group of us on pilgrimage sat at the sea of Galilee one afternoon, actually guided by another Franciscan, and, as we sat, he quietly read the story of the apostles going fishing, Jesus on the shore, the excitement of recognition, Jesus cooking the fish and sharing the meal – and then the Israeli jets flew thunderously overhead and we were back in the 20th century!

I would guess that many questions about favourite resurrection narratives would go to Luke 24, joining the disciples on the road to Emmaus and encountering Jesus. It is a good story. We can identify with the two dismayed disciples, broken expectations, the chance encounter with a stranger, his opening their eyes, their wanting him to stay, the breaking of the bread, the realisation that their hearts were burning within them as the stranger spoke and they recognised him.

Someone once alerted me that a way of appreciating this Emmaus journey was to see it in the context of the Eucharist. Perhaps it is too fanciful to think that the Lukan community made this link between the way they celebrated the Eucharist, their remembrance of him.

But it is worth pointing out the links. The two disciples (and we remember the story often told of Cardinal Martini visiting Melbourne and host, Dorothy Lee, suggesting that one of the disciples could have been a woman – and everyone taken aback at first when the Cardinal insisted that this could not be! And he went on to explain that never in the Gospel does Jesus rebuke a woman for her lack of faith!)

The two set out on their journey and are immediately challenged by the accompanying stranger to examine their conscience, so to speak, about their hopes and fears because of Jesus' death – a penitential rite. He then goes on to explain the Scriptures to them, all the passages about himself and the fact that the Christ should suffer and die – the Liturgy of the Word. Jesus had celebrated his Last Supper, given the gift of his body and his blood which was to be shed the next day. They welcome Jesus to the table. He breaks the bread – communion – and, as he vanishes, they eagerly set out to proclaim the good news of resurrection to the apostles in Jerusalem. Not a very quiet, 'Let us go in the peace of Christ'.

End language!

Jonah: Odd Prophet Out

There are several references to Jonah in the Gospels; Jesus even suggests that Jonas's sojourn in the belly of the whale is a dramatic sign of his resurrection: 'And a greater than Jonah is here!' (Matthew 12:38). Jonah was also very popular in the art of the early church, appropriately sculpted on many a sarcophagus, the hope of the resurrection for the person being interred. Which makes Jonah something of a serious character. But in fact, he is not... not quite.

Back in my early years of seminary studies, part of the wonderful experience was the opening up of the Old Testament. I can't remember what attracted me to Jonah but I do know that I wrote a very extensive essay about him and received a good mark!

But the main discovery about Jonah and his book of prophecy – certainly a book unlike any of the other major or minor prophets – is that it is something of a comedy. It is a satiric comedy, especially at Jonah's expense. Now while there is a lot of action, a lot of drama, even a lot of melodrama in the Jewish Scriptures, there is minimal comedy. Jonah contributes to closing the comedy gap. (And I always feel a certain dismay when this section of Jonah is read during the liturgy, especially in Lent – it is voiced mostly in the most sonorous and solemn of voices, not at all representing the way in which it was written. The immediate emotion is: 'Lighten up').

Jonah's initial encounter with God's voice is the briefest prophetic call: 'Go to Nineveh, the great city, and inform them that their wickedness has become known to me', but what is Jonah's immediate reaction? He decides to run away from Yahweh, hurries down to Joppa, finds a ship, pays his fare (an edifying detail), goes aboard 'to get away from Yahweh'. And this is only verses 1-3!

Actually, the rest of the chapter is quite exciting: Yahweh unleashing a great storm, the ship threatening to break up, the sailors all beginning to pray, jettisoning the cargo – Jonah, however, had gone below and is lying down in the hold and has fallen fast asleep. The sailors do all the praying but, when challenged, Jonah is arrogantly assertive, 'I am a Hebrew, and I worship Yahweh the God of heaven, who made the sea and the land'.

Then a sudden conversion experience – Jonah willing to take the blame, to be tossed overboard. We are no longer surprised: the great fish, and Jonah spending three days and three nights (no wonder the Gospel communities recognised him as a sign of Jesus' tomb experience). But then, Jonah excels himself and prays a psalm that could easily find its place amongst the other 150. So Jonah is not a lost cause. And the author succinctly notes at the end of the beautiful psalm: 'Yahweh spoke to the fish, which then vomited Jonah onto the shore'.

This is certainly not sounding like any of the other calls of the prophets! This has to be read with tongue-in-cheek. Or a recognition that the author was composing a variation on prophetic activity, tongue-in-cheek.

God is good. Jonah gets a second chance. Start again. Same call, same mission. But a bit more detail about Nineveh to remind Jonah of the importance of what God was asking of him: 'Nineveh was a great city beyond compare; it took three days to cross it'. Jonah then makes a journey part of the way, one day. And, in the translation of the *Jerusalem Bible*, 'only forty days more and Nineveh is going to be destroyed', 11 words in total in English, the briefest, most succinct, prophetic message – and what happens? What can one say but instant conversion! Belief in God, fast proclaimed, everyone in sackcloth, the king rising from his throne, taking off his robe, wearing sackcloth, sitting down in ashes: men and beasts, herds and flocks, a fast; they must not eat, they must not drink water. All are to put on sackcloth and call on God with all their might, that everyone renounce their evil behaviour and the wicked things they have done. The king hopes that God will relent, renounce his burning wrath. And, the book continues, God seems to be very pleased with what he saw, relented and did not inflict on them the disaster which he had threatened.

If only the book of Jonah ended here, it would be an ultimate triumph after the initial humiliating failure. So how does Jonah celebrate this extraordinary religious experience?

If there was satire in the first chapter in Jonah's behaviour and his whale of an experience, there is even more, and at Jonah's expense! We are certainly into satiric comedy by this stage of the book, very short book as it is. Jonah's reaction – indignation, falling into a rage, complaining to God that this is exactly what he thought would happen when he was still at home and which is why he refused to go to Nineveh and fled to Tarshish. Then a fatal confession: 'I knew that you were a God of tenderness and compassion, slow to anger, rich in graciousness, relenting from evil'. And the consequence of this – the complaint that God should take Jonah's life because he might as well be dead. No religious sensitivity at all.

And so the full prophetic message is preached to Jonah himself. God asks him if he has any right to be angry. Jonah sulks, and the tender and compassionate God feels a bit sorry for his prophet and arranges for a shelter where Jonah could sit in the shade to see what would happen to the city.

Who says that God doesn't have a mischievous sense of humour? He still wants to teach Jonah the error of his non-prophetic ways. God arranges the castor-oil plant to give more shade for Jonah and 'to soothe his ill humour'. Jonah is delighted. Then the *pièce de résistance*: at dawn, the next day, God arranges that a worm should attack the castor-oil plant and it withers. The sun rose, God arranged a scorching east wind, the sun beating down so hard on Jonah's (bald) head that he was overcome and begged for death, once again stating he might as well be dead as go on living.

And the moral of this prophetic satire: God reprimanding Jonah for being upset and angry about a castor-oil plant. It cost him no labour, Jonah did not make it grow, and it sprouted on a night and perished the next day. And the phenomenon of God's speech that ends in midsentence: 'Am I not to feel sorry for Nineveh, the great city, in which there are more than 120,000 people who cannot tell their right hand from the left, to say nothing of all the animals...'

End of inspired Hebrew Scriptures book.

So, some Hebrew comedy. If only there were more... But in his quiet way, Jesus took up the challenge.

Jesus as Stand-up Comedian

That chapter heading is something of an attention-grabber! I do remember some eyebrows being raised in the past at a mention of this. But the title makes something of a point that is not always made. Maybe we have been affected by some the recent stand-up comics, frequently opting for the distasteful, relying on expletives that are a turnoff rather than a humorous turn-on. Maybe the satire is too savage. But the best stand-up comics know their audiences, know how to cheer them, know how to make them smile, laugh. And get the point!

Perhaps you have read the novel, seen the film or the television miniseries of Umberto Eco's *The Name of the Rose*. It is a mediaeval story, a murder mystery in a monastery, a severe community where some of the monks were against laughter, philosophically because of its disruption to order, religiously because laughter had the power to undermine authority.

There were some authorities that Jesus wanted to undermine. There were the excesses of the Scribes and Pharisees, the non-spiritual scepticism of the Sadducees, the complacency of the rich...

But it is not to say that Jesus was uproarious in his sense of humour. There is no major emphasis in the Gospels to indicate that Jesus laughed. Surely he smiled in his dealings in drawing the little children to him. Surely when he received hospitality from friends like Martha and Mary, in their home, he relaxed and smiled. People were attracted to him, they felt welcome. While he could definitely speak some stern words (once again to those Scribes and Pharisees and some sharp alerts, even to the apostles), Jesus was a humane man.

And when he spoke to those near him, when he spoke to the big crowds, he knew them well, their day-to-day lives, their practical concerns, the deeper worries, difficulties in relationships, how to make ends meet. So he could adapt his teaching to speak to those concerns. And he knew how to touch them with his words, even to make them smile, even to make them laugh.

And how did Jesus manifest this comic style?

One occasion that springs to mind comes from Luke 11. Jesus is alerting his audience to serious themes, the heading in the *Jerusalem Bible*: Effective Prayer. And the way Jesus makes his point – and it sounds as though he is particularly thinking of fathers – is to appeal to their common sense: whether they would offer their children a stone instead of bread (echoes of the temptation in the desert), or hand them a snake instead of a fish, or a scorpion instead of an egg! And the point being: if you know how to treat your children well, so much more does God your loving father.

What about some of the examples in Matthew – Jesus' Sermon on the Mount? Again, he is into comparisons, but this time with the savvy of building security. The story of the man who built his hand on sand: rain came down, floods rose, gales blew and hurled themselves against that house... And it fell; what a fall it had! Jesus bluntly refers to this man is stupid.

And certainly Jesus did have a way with words. I'm not sure I've heard many preachers offering such images: 'Do not give dogs what is holy, and do not throw your pearls in front of pigs, they may trample them and then turn on you and tear you to pieces'. That advice certainly made its impact and we still refer to pearls before swine.

And Jesus could play a situation for its comic, sometimes ironic effect, especially if he had a participating audience. He met something of his match in the encounter with the Canaanite woman, pleading for him to heal her daughter, and his disdainful-sounding comment that he was sent only to the lost sheep of the House of Israel. He laid it on a bit thickly when he then told her that it was not fair to take the children's food and throw it to the household dogs. Her retort was quick and smart: but even house dogs can eat the scraps that fall from their master's table. And Jesus applauded her faith – and fulfilled her request for healing.

Some of the parables are played for smiles. What about the unjust judge and the widow who keeps coming, persevering, persisting, pestering him until he gives in and admits how tough her persuasion was. Or, sometimes Jesus is provocative in what some movie classifiers used to note, 'unnecessary offensive detail'! It really wasn't essential or even proper to refer to pigs in the parable of the Prodigal Son, let alone the son's starving and craving the pigs' food. And the Pharisees don't always come out of the parables well. What about the story of the Pharisee and the tax collector, the wide gulf from the front of the synagogue to the back where each was placed and, with the wily translation, the Pharisees said his prayers – to himself!

As has been said, Jesus knew his audience, knew their concerns, spoke to their experience, and sometimes made them smile.

Might be good if you jotted down the next time you notice Jesus and the touch of the stand-up comedian.

Jesus Splashes his Mother

Over the centuries, Christians have constantly imagined what Jesus might have been like. The above title reference will come up later. (Those who have seen *The Passion of the Christ* will remember.)

In his *Spiritual Exercises*, St Ignatius Loyola invites us to enter into the Gospel scene – a 'composition of place' – imagining ourselves in the Gospel (and the question of how close we are to Jesus or how far distant). And after the Gospels were written, it was not long before alternative, fanciful imaginings began to be written down – Apocryphal Gospels, as they were called. Many decades ago, we were told some of these stories in religion classes at school, the spider weaving a web while the holy family was hiding in a cave escaping to Egypt so that they would not be discovered by the pursuing soldiers, or stories about Dismas, the robber, who had his moment of grace on Calvary as the Good Thief. Legends, associated with the saints, began to proliferate – St Christopher, the Christ-bearer, carrying Jesus across a river. And the stories took dramatic shape in the Middle Ages – the writing and the performance of the Miracle Plays, often on the steps of the Cathedral. There are many elaborations of stories about the history of biblical characters, especially Mary Magdalene (and all the way down to Dan Brown and *The Da Vinci Code*).

These imaginative stories were embellished as the visual arts developed, especially during the Renaissance: Mary, with Jesus as a child and his cousin John the Baptist. There was Jesus with his apostles, and especially, the Judases.

And there have been some wonderful stories in our films. There is a fine sequence in *King of Kings* with a visit by Jesus to his cousin John in prison. But in the late 1960s and into the 70s, despite precedents from Johan Sebastian Bach and his St Matthew's Passion, there was something of a shock when the Gospels were imagined as Rock Operas – *Jesus Christ Superstar* and *Godspell* – which every schoolchild in our capital cities was taken to see, either on stage or on screen. Some of the songs from *Godspell* (Prepare Ye the Way of the Lord) found their way into our hymn books. And many a Christian imagination found it difficult at first to associate Jesus with the appellation, Superstar! I always like to single out one song in *Jesus Christ Superstar* as highlighting the imagination – Jesus starting his agony in the Garden of Gethsemane but beginning to climb the cliff face, becoming more intense, reaching the top and emitting a primal scream before settling down to his acceptance of the Father's will.

And our filmmakers began to rearrange the Gospel texts, interlinking different texts. One that I would recommend is Zeffirelli's narration of the parable of the Prodigal Son in *Jesus of Nazareth*, with Jesus being criticised, as Luke's Gospel says, because he dined with the tax collectors and prostitutes. Here it is the dinner hosted by Matthew, the tax collector. Peter, resentful of Matthew and his taxes, refuses to go in but listening to Robert Powell's wonderful narration, he does come inside, like the older son of the parable, and reconciles with Matthew. (I sometimes wonder whether St Luke in Heaven wonders 'why didn't I think of that?')

No, I haven't forgotten the reference to Jesus splashing his mother! However, five years before Mel Gibson introduced his flashback into the middle of the Passion, there was another delightful incident in *Jesus* of Jesus splashing, this time his fellow apostles. Jesus and the Twelve come into a square, a beggar asks for money, then begins to play music, Jesus beginning to dance (and Thomas scowling as he is dragged to accompany Jesus). When Jesus has had enough, the beginning of a sweat, he goes up to the fountain in the square, takes a drink, and, when the others come up, he splashes and starts a water fight. Not quite the Gospel text!

– but audiences enjoy it, a reminder of the down-to-earth, everyday Jesus.

While watching the grim narration of *The Passion of the Christ*, it was something of a surprise to find that there were quite a number of gentle flashbacks – the call of Mary Magdalene, the horror of the nailing broken by a quiet flashback to the Last Supper. And with Mary at the foot of the cross, there are flashbacks to Jesus' childhood, Jesus stumbling and Mary hurrying after to pick him up. But also, Jesus working as a carpenter, making a table for his mother, the legs not even, having a lean, and, as he prepares for his meal, splashing his mother from the sink. Many audiences don't remember these flashbacks so overwhelmed were they by the Passion – but Mel Gibson was trying to be creative, reminding us who Jesus was, even as he was suffering and dying.

Once again, there may be episodes in the Jesus films that you have seen which may have made you appreciate Jesus as a person, even though it was not exactly a Gospel story.

Imaging the Tempter

What are our images of Satan, images that help us appreciate the presence of malevolence in our world, the image of the devil?

Many of us go back to the book of Genesis, the tempting of Adam and Eve, their fall. And images of the new Eve, Mary, in the statues, her foot on the serpent.

I would like to suggest some images from the Jesus films, often quite striking, mainly during the principal appearance of the devil, the temptations in the desert.

In *Jesus* (1999), a scarlet-clad woman first appears in the desert and taunts Jesus with his human condition, inviting him to empty himself of his divinity, of his Father. Actor Jeroen Krabbé then appears, playing Satan dressed in a black suit and, again, offering Jesus tempting modern images of power, of contemporary poverty and suffering, that resonate with a contemporary audience. He tells Jesus it has only just begun. He returns even more vengeful for the agony in the garden.

It is in the agony in the garden and the return of Satan that the drama is intense. Jesus says that he must face his death as a man, and falls on his face on the ground. 'I am afraid. I can't endure this.' Satan tells Jesus that this is the final act, that there will be no reprieve from the Father. Satan also relishes his sadistic description of crucifixion and the slow suffocation. Jesus' answer is that in his death, 'through me God will reveal his love for mankind'. While Satan condemns God as 'heartless', asking Jesus what kind of God would allow such poverty and war, Jesus offers him the answer about God giving us the gift of free will, that God is not a dictator. 'So this is what they choose', Satan retorts.

At the opening of the film, Jesus has a dream (or vision), a kind of recurring dream that takes him into the future, glimpsing sin and evil over the centuries. In the sequence of the temptations in the desert, Jesus sees images of contemporary poverty and hunger, but in his agony, he walks with Satan through history with even more detail of Crusades (onslaughts in the name of Jesus), the burning of a witch (in the name of Our Lord), and finally their walking through the gunfire in a bombed town in World War I.

Finally, Jesus tells Satan that he will not die alone. He will be with his Father and 'those who want to will find in me the strength to love to the end'.

It was with Mel Gibson's *The Passion of the Christ*, that the appearances of Satan made an impact. Gibson's words about the devil offer us a challenge. 'I believe the devil is real, but I don't believe he shows up too often with horns and smoke and a forked tail. The devil is smarter than that. Evil is alluring, attractive. It looks almost normal, almost good – but not quite.

'... what I tried to do with the devil in the film... The actor's face is symmetric, beautiful in a certain sense, but not completely. For example, we shaved her eyebrows. Then we shot her almost in slow motion so you don't see her blink – that's not normal. We dubbed in a man's voice in Gethsemane even though the actor is a woman... That's what evil is about, taking something that's good and twisting it a little bit.'

And Satan carrying the ugly baby? 'Again, it's evil distorting what's good. What is more tender and beautiful than a mother and a child? So the devil takes that and distorts it just a little bit. Instead of a normal mother and child, you have an androgynous figure holding a 40-year-old 'baby' with hair on his back. It is weird, it is shocking, it's almost too much – just like turning Jesus over to continue scourging him on his chest is shocking and almost too much, which is the exact moment when this appearance of the devil and the baby takes place.' (Mark Moring, *Christianity Today*, 1 March 2004)

Satan appears to Jesus praying in Gethsemane. Satan tries to deceive Jesus by warning him of the dangers of dying to atone the sins of humanity. This would cause God's will to fail. Jesus ignores this and continues to pray. However, a serpent emerges from Satan's black cloak and slithers towards Jesus. He notices this in time and crushes it with his foot. Satan promptly vanishes from the scene, to reappear at key moments, at the scourging, with Pilate, at the cross. Gibson also signals God's grief – after the death of Jesus, the camera seems to zoom up to the heavens and then a single drop of water – like God's teardrop –. splashes to earth.

The South African *Son of Man* brings the Gospel into the 21st century in the conflicts of that country. The film opens with the Temptations. Jesus and Satan are black men, Satan dressed in warrior clothes, with an ominous hoof-stick machete. The setting is sandy and rocky desert terrain, but it is on the coast. A rock for bread is picked up from the ground. Satan's invitation to accept the kingdoms of this world takes place on a hill above a beach where Jesus walks away. They stand on the cliff top while Satan asks Jesus to throw himself over. Jesus walks away. The third time, they sit as Satan asks for worship. But Jesus roughly shoves him down the hill. Satan asserts that it is his world. Jesus retorts that it is his world and he will return. The appearance of Jesus for non-Africans is arresting. He is covered in white paint which, fifteen minutes later, we find is part of his initiation ceremony as a man. The imagining of the temptations as part of this initiation rite makes good sense.

And there is also the danger of a fundamentalist reading of the Gospels.

In the Protestant-financed, *Jesus* (later re-edited for evangelical purposes, *The Jesus Project*), the devil is visualised literally as a snake, slithering and hissing through the rocks in his encounter with Jesus. However, when the battle of the scripture texts between the devil and Jesus is heard, the devil's voice is one of the plummiest-toned, beautifully-enunciated English voices you could hear. Jesus may usually have been seen and heard as a middle-class Englishman, but the devil has moved upper-class!

Mary Mother, Mary Prophet

When you are asked to pray about Jesus' human life, which Gospel do you go to? If you like stories, you probably go to Luke's Gospel, the story of the Annunciation to Mary and her consent. If you like themes, you may well go to John's Gospel, the prologue about the Word and the Word becoming flesh.

I'm going to suggest some reflection on both Gospels. With John's Gospel, I would like to focus on Mary as the mother of Jesus. With Luke's Gospel, by contrast, I would like to focus on Mary and what we might call her 'prophetic' role.

John chapter 1 brings to the conclusion of its wonderful hymn, 'In the beginning was the Word, and the Word was with God, and the Word was God... And the Word was made flesh and dwelt amongst us'. But then the Gospel goes on to say that the Word, Jesus, 'is nearest to the Father's heart and has made God known'.

We know there is a focus on Mary as mother in John's Gospel, twice. There she is with Jesus at the wedding feast in Cana, suggesting to Jesus that he do a sign, not ordering him, rather commanding those attending to fill the vessels with water. The change was the first of Jesus' signs and his disciples believed in him. Mary, so to speak, created/initiated the sign. Mary's second appearance in John's Gospel is at the foot of the cross – Mary, the grieving mother, committed to the care of the beloved disciple. To the beloved disciple, and so us, and we in turn entrusted to Mary who becomes mother of the Church.

Mary, mother of Jesus, mother of Jesus' heart, brings the very heart of God into our world.

Perhaps you have not been thinking of Mary as a prophet. But the prophets of Hebrew history were specially chosen, had a special experience, a distinctive encounter with God's presence, were entrusted with God's very word to communicate it with its invitation, with its challenge, with its dynamic power.

This is particularly the case in Luke's narrative. Mary of Nazareth, betrothed to Joseph of the house of David, is singled out by the messenger of the final times, Gabriel (from the book of Daniel), is asked to listen to God's word, God's promises, the fulfilment of Covenant promises, in her son. Mary's word is 'yes'. She conceives the word. She nurtures the word in her womb. She gives birth to the word. She is in the line of the prophets – and their fulfilment.

I don't know whether you have ever made a comparison between the prophet Jeremiah and Mary. A theological and devotional language names Mary from the first moment of her conception as sinless, the Immaculate Conception. But as we go back to Jeremiah chapter 1, we actually find God using this same kind of language concerning the prophet, that before Jeremiah was in the womb, God loved him. And the young Jeremiah was reminded of his mission even though he pleaded an excuse by saying that he was too young. God seemed to be a bit more determined with Jeremiah and he tells him to stop saying that he is a child. And then, vigorously, he says, 'Look, I am putting my words in your mouth. You have my word'. And then, the command: GO!

We know that it wasn't always easy for Jeremiah; he was not always listened to, he was persecuted, even thrown down a well. But his constant prayer was, 'I commit my cause to you'. Jeremiah had the privilege to speak the prophetic words of God's love, God's everlasting love, and, personalising it, so many centuries before the coming of Jesus, 'I am constant in my affection for you'. And through Jeremiah, God promised that the law would no longer be written on tablets of stone but would be embedded there in our very hearts of flesh. We would know God's love intimately.

Which is what Mary did. And she suffered. And she committed her cause to God. And her word, Jesus, gave us the law of love, loving one another as he loved us, laying down his life, day by day and then in death, for all of us whom he no longer calls servants but friends.

We can also note that this idea of God loving someone in the womb is found in the second Servant Song (Isaiah 49: I) – 'God called me before I was born. From my mother's womb he pronounced my name'. And we might remember Elizabeth's words to Mary about John leaping in her womb at the presence of Mary pregnant with Jesus.

I would like to add a personal note. My religious congregation honours Mary with the title Our Lady of the Sacred Heart. Thinking of John's words about Jesus, the Word, nearest to the father's heart and now made known, and Jeremiah's expression of God's love, constant affection, deep in our hearts, I think our founder, Jules Chevalier, was right in his insight in honouring Mary the mother and prophet as Our Lady of the Sacred Heart.

Mary Growing Older

When we listen to Gospel stories about the mother of Jesus, are we conscious of how old she is? Or, as with so many people, does she seem ageless? We have to remind ourselves that Mary ages during Jesus' life, is portrayed at different stages of her life in the Gospels. No problem in remembering the very young and pregnant Mary, the Mary giving birth to Jesus, in the stable at Bethlehem, the visit of the Magi, and the desperate flight into Egypt and later return to Nazareth. In fact, we have to remind ourselves that Mary is twelve years older at the time that Jesus chooses to be lost in the temple, the time of his bar mitzvah. And do we make the adjustment to Mary thirty years older or so at Cana, at the foot of the cross, gathered with the disciples in prayer in the upper room, awaiting the coming of the Spirit?

How many of us contemplate Mary growing older, especially the older Mary in John's Gospel?

We have a visual tradition of images of Mary and it would be fascinating to check with ourselves how influenced we are by Christian art. Perhaps we could remind ourselves. In the first centuries of the church, Mary did not feature much. It was after the acceptance of Christianity in the Roman Empire that she made appearances. Many of her images were in the beautiful mosaics in the apses of basilicas, a very stylised Mary, an iconic Mary, in herself, in relationship to Jesus. This was important in the fifth century when the Council of Ephesus defined Mary as the mother of God.

In the art of the Middle Ages, in frescoes, in statues, she is situated more in the Gospel stories. But of course, it is in the Renaissance that paintings and statues of Mary abound. These were the centuries of the Madonna. We could highlight Raphael as the master painter of young and beautiful Madonnas, Madonnas with Jesus the child. For statues, the obvious choice is Michelangelo. And the even more obvious choice is Mary with her dead son, the Pietà. And this tradition continued, especially in Italy.

After the Reformation, we find the Catholic imagination of Mary; Protestants very wary of such images, Oliver Cromwell in a campaign of destroying images.

Those of us not as young as we used to be remember growing up with more pious images of Mary – Our Lady of Lourdes, then Our Lady of Fatima, Mary in blue, Mary in white, Mary standing alone, or with the infant Jesus, on pedestals or in niches in every parish church. And this was reproduced in the numerous holy cards that found their place in our prayer books and missals. Mary is always young, sometimes looking to heaven, maternal towards her baby. (The danger was that we had many kitsch images of Mary.)

With the coming of movie images, there were better possibilities even if the initial screen images of Mary were reflections of the plaster statues and the pious holy cards.

I would like to make some recommendations. Perhaps the casting of Mary in the early Jesus films, in the 1960s, relied too much on the impact of the film star portraying Mary – Dorothy McGuire, Siobhan McKenna, *King of Kings, Greatest Story ever Told*. But if you would like a contrast, please consider Pier Paolo Pasolini's *Gospel According to Matthew*, in which he cast his mother, an elderly woman, presented in Italian style, all grieving and gesticulating on Calvary. At the time, I remember seeing a statue of Our Lady of Sorrows in Naples, the same overwrought Mary, with, literally, seven large swords piercing and protruding from her heart. Cultural differences! And, speaking of cultural differences, my friend, reviewer Jan Epstein, noted that Mary in Mel Gibson's *Passion of the Christ*, was a quiet, controlled, grieving mother – not at all in the manner of an image of the reactions of a Jewish mother!

Olivia Hussey in *Jesus of Nazareth* does show us the ageing Mary, the very young maiden of Nazareth, the more mature mother of Jesus searching for him, and, transformed, older during the passion. One of the advantages of the screen presence of Mary is that she is not a statue, we see her in real life, a flesh and blood person, hear her words, respond to her body language.

One sequence which beautifully mirrors a statue is found in the 1999 *Jesus*. Mary is played by Jacqueline Bissett and, when Jesus is taken down from the cross, he is laid in his mother's lap, and there is the visual of the Pietà, with Andrew Lloyd Webber's *Requiem* plaintiff as background score. (Interestingly, for the anointing of Jesus before his burial, it is Mary who takes charge, the women helping with the anointing, and then Mary going on her knees as Jesus is buried.)

One image of Mary, older, where she looks definitely matronly, not just older, a mature woman, a somewhat heavy woman, in command at Cana, a middle-aged mother at the foot of the cross is seen in the complete text version, *The Gospel of John*.

A strikingly different image of Mary, a black Mary, can be seen in the South African *Son of Man* – especially in her singing the *Magnificat* in the immediate aftermath of the Annunciation.

If the tradition of paintings and statues has influenced our listening to the gospel, I would hope that this new a tradition of moving images would be an even stronger – more realistic? – impact on our listening, our prayer, our contemplation.

My Jesus Film/your Jesus Film

'My Jesus film.'

Perhaps you could discover more about your appreciation for Jesus by doing as I was asked to do: write something about which film is your favourite Jesus film – and why? I had to write for a reading public. Your readership might just be yourself.

This was a Holy Week request for an Easter Supplement in a Catholic paper. The Jesus film that has meant most to me is Franco Zeffirelli's *Jesus of Nazareth*. I also have a soft spot for the animated story, *The Miracle Maker*, as well as the lesser known 1999 film, *Jesus*, made for television and featuring Jeremy Sisto as one of the most acceptable and agreeable Jesus-figures, capturing the very human Jesus, but also the divine in the human.

But *Jesus of Nazareth* is the favourite.

Two personal experiences. Robert Powell came to Australia in 1978 to promote the film. Catholic Communications, Sydney, decided to make a television program and I was invited to review the film and then interview Robert Powell. In those leisurely days, the floor crew had time off for lunch – just as we were about to start the interview. Off they went. The good news was that we had forty-five minutes talking to the actor. The bad news was that the publicist wanted him for his next appointment just as the crew were coming back.

But God was on our side. The lunchtime discussion was very moving. Powell told us how he had given three years of his life to *Jesus of Nazareth*: a year in preparation and rehearsal, a year in filming and a year in travelling and promotion. He explained that he was brought up as an Anglican but had not attended church very much. What had been very significant for him – in the light of his memories of Eucharistic celebrations – was how awed he felt during the Last Supper scenes. He had to become Jesus saying the words that he had so often heard in his past. He had to communicate the profound mystery as well as help audiences appreciate how Jesus was giving the gift of himself as he anticipated his fearful passion and death. He told us that this had made a profound impression on him.

I was pleased to be able to tell him how his speaking of the parable of the Prodigal Son was one of the great moments of film-making for me. The way that he spoke, the way that he looked, the way that he told that most wonderful of Jesus' stories was just right.

And the interview? Robert Powell is a gentleman. When the publicist urged him that it was necessary to go, I saw him put his hand behind his back and give an indication to the publicist with his fingers, either 'wait a bit' or 'give me five minutes more'. We got our interview.

The second personal experience is this: a retreat experience. One of the most memorable evenings consisted in sitting in the dark while one of the retreat leaders quietly retold the Gospel stories in his own way. On the wall he projected a series of slides from *Jesus of Nazareth*. We listened. We looked. We contemplated. Robert Powell was the face and the gestures of Jesus. For many people in the 1980s, Robert Powell was Jesus, so popular was the film and the television series, so popular were the slides and the books.

What is it about *Jesus of Nazareth* that makes it so memorable?

One of the reasons that I like it so much is that it does not simply use the Gospel text as a screenplay. It combines Gospel text with narrative written for the film by Catholic novelist Anthony Burgess (best known as the author of *A Clockwork Orange*). Peter Ustinov's Herod, for instance, is able to explain the historical situation in Palestine. Zeffirelli and Burgess also create a fictitious character, the secretary of the Sanhedrin, played by Ian Holm. He is able to fill in the background so that the audience understands better the social and religious implications of what Jesus says and does, why the authorities begin to hate Jesus and plot against him.

Three examples of how *Jesus of Nazareth* works so well for me.

Jesus is at Simon's house for dinner. The Pharisees discuss the greatest commandments, telling Jesus he is too strict. Jesus praises Joseph of Arimathea for his insights. Simon, upset, asks, 'Who is my neighbour?' Instead of telling the parable of the Good Samaritan, Jesus is disturbed by the sinful woman who comes in, weeps for her sins and anoints Jesus' feet. When you see this scene, watch Robert Powell's face. As you listen, you will realise that he acts it as if he had not rehearsed. He is genuinely surprised, moved and full of genuine compassion.

The setting for the Prodigal Son is also well imagined. Jesus has called Matthew to follow him. As tax collector, Matthew has been extorting money from Peter and the other fishermen. When Jesus goes to Matthew's banquet with the sinners, Peter refuses. When he does relent and stands outside the door, he hears the parable, realises that he is the hard, older brother and comes inside, asking Jesus how often he should forgive.

As mentioned earlier in this book, perhaps, St Luke in heaven looking down at Zefferelli's film structure saying, 'Why didn't I think of that?'!

Also noted earlier, on the way to Calvary, a voiceover recites the fourth Servant Song from Isaiah (the song that is read in Good Friday liturgy). The voice is that of Laurence Olivier, so it sounds solemn and clear. But whom did Olivier play? Nicodemus. Nicodemus knew his scriptures, came to Jesus and then took care of his burial. A cinematic way of gathering together rich biblical themes.

These are some of the reasons why *Jesus of Nazareth* means so much to me. And your Jesus film?

And then...

Over to you to keep exploring Jesus according to the Scriptures.